Ulrich Renz / Barbara Brinkmann

Xewnên xweş, gurê piçûk

Schlaf gut, kleiner Wolf

Pirtûka bi wêneyan bi du zimanan

Werger:

Brahim Shexo, Osnabrück, Germany (Kurdî / Kurmancî)

sefa

Little Wolf would like to meet you at his home:

www.childrens-books-bilingual.com

"Şev xweş, Tim! Lêgera xwe emê sibe berdewam bikin.
Nûke razê!"

"Gute Nacht, Tim! Wir suchen morgen weiter.
Jetzt schlaf schön!"

Ji derve tarî ye.

Draußen ist es schon dunkel.

Tim li wir çi dike balo?

Was macht Tim denn da?

Bi alî derve de dire, li hêwana leystikê.

Qey li çi yê xwe digere li wir?

Er geht raus, zum Spielplatz.

Was sucht er da?

Gurê xwey piçûk!
Bêyî wîya nikare xew bike.

Den kleinen Wolf!
Ohne den kann er nicht schlafen.

Kî li vê derê ye?

Wer kommt denn da?

Marie!

Li goga xwe digere.

Marie!

Die sucht ihren Ball.

Û Tobi îcar li çi digere?

Und was sucht Tobi?

Li ekskavatorê xwe.

Seinen Bagger.

Û Nala?

Und was sucht Nala?

Li bêbîka xwe.

Ihre Puppe.

Gerek niha zarok xew bikin, ne wilo?

Pisîkê pir matmayî dinêre.

Müssen die Kinder nicht ins Bett?

Die Katze wundert sich sehr.

Û niha kî tê?

Wer kommt denn jetzt?

Dayik û bavê Tim!

Bêyî wîya nikarin xew bikin.

Die Mama und der Papa von Tim!

Ohne ihren Tim können sie nicht schlafen.

Û wa bîhtir kes tên! Bavê Marie.

Kalkê Tobi. Û dayika Nala.

Und da kommen noch mehr! Der Papa von Marie.

Der Opa von Tobi. Und die Mama von Nala.

Niha zû bi alî textên xwe!

Jetzt aber schnell ins Bett!

"Şev baş, Tim! Sibe pêdivî nema pê heye em lêgera xwe berdewam bikin."

"Gute Nacht, Tim!
Morgen müssen wir nicht mehr suchen."

"Xewnên xweş, gurê piçûk!"

"Schlaf gut, kleiner Wolf!"

More about me ...

  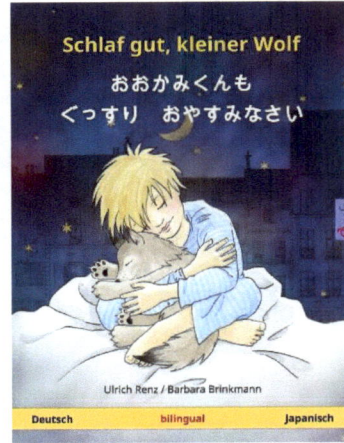 

   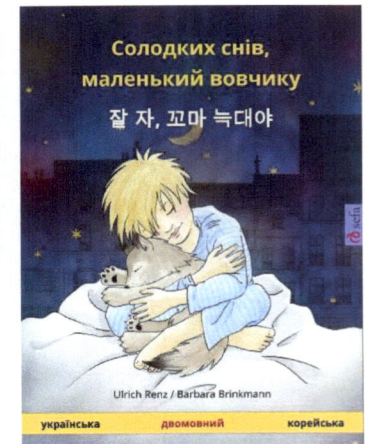

A Children's Book
for the Global Village

"Sleep Tight, Little Wolf" is a multilingual picture book for the ever growing number of children who face the challenge – and the opportunity – of living with different cultures and languages. Their families may have been displaced to another country as refugees. Or their parents may have chosen the life of expats, working for a global company or an NGO. Perhaps it may merely have been love that brought together two people from different world regions who don't even speak the same language.

Migration and ensuing multilingualism is a global megatrend of our days. Ever more children are born away from their parents' home countries, and are balancing between the languages of their mother, their father, their grandparents, and their peers. "Sleep Tight, Little Wolf" is meant to help bridge the language divides that cross more and more families, neighborhoods and kindergartens in the globalized world. This is a global picture book – coming to you in more than 50 languages and all conceivable bilingual combinations of them.

www.childrens-books-bilingual.com

Bilingual Children's Books - in any language you want

Home	Authors	The Little Wolf	About

Welcome to the **Little Wolf's Language Wizard!**

Tell me, first of all, in which language you want me to work for you. English or German?

English ▼ | Go!

Now just choose the two languages in which you want to read to your children:

Language 1:

Please choose... ▼

Language 2:

no 2nd language ▼

Go!

Learn more about the Little Wolf project at *www.childrens-books-bilingual.com.* At the heart of this website you will find what we call the "Little Wolf's Language Wizard". It contains more than 50 languages and any of their bilingual combinations: Just select, in a simple drop-down-menu, the two languages in which you'd like to read the story to your child – and the book is instantly made available, ready for order as an ebook download or as a printed edition.

As time goes by ...

... the little ones grow older, and start to read on their own. Here is Little Wolf's recommendation to them:

BO & FRIENDS

Smart detective stories for smart children

Reading age: 10 + - www.bo-and-friends.com

Wie die Zeit vergeht ...

Irgendwann sind aus den süßen Kleinen süße Große geworden
– die jetzt sogar selber lesen können. Der kleine Wolf empfiehlt:

MOTTE & CO

Kinderkrimis zum Mitdenken

Lesealter ab 10 – www.motte-und-co.de

About the authors

Ulrich Renz was born in Stuttgart, Germany, in 1960. After studying French literature in Paris he graduated from medical school in Lübeck and worked as head of a scientific publishing company. He is now a writer of non-fiction books as well as children's fiction books. – www.ulrichrenz.de

Barbara Brinkmann was born in Munich, Germany, in 1969. She grew up in the foothills of the Alps and studied architecture and medicine for a while in Munich. She now works as a freelance graphic artist, illustrator and writer. – www.bcbrinkmann.com